PRAYER PATHS

Mark Link, s.j.

Search for Serenity and God in an Age of Stress

TABOR®
PUBLISHING
Allen, Texas

IMPRIMI POTEST
Robert A. Wild, S.J.

NIHIL OBSTAT
Rev. Glenn D. Gardner
Censor Librorum

IMPRIMATUR
Most Rev. Charles Grahmann
Bishop of Dallas

August 16, 1990

The *Nihil Obstat* and *Imprimatur* are official declarations that the work contains nothing contrary to Faith and Morals. It is not implied thereby that those granting the *Nihil Obstat* and *Imprimatur* agree with the contents, statements, or opinions expressed.

Unless otherwise noted, all Scripture quotations are from the *Good News Bible*, in Today's English Version. Copyright © American Bible Society 1966, 1971, 1976. Used by permission.

CALLIGRAPHY
Bob Niles

PHOTO CREDITS
Gene Ahrens   40
Algimantas Kezys   16
Jean-Claude Lejeune   cover, vi, 8, 22, 30, 50, 68, 78, 86, 106, 114, 134, 152
Mark Link   58, 96, 124, 142

COVER PHOTO
Hand-color tinted by The Art Source

Send all inquiries to:
Tabor Publishing
One DLM Park
Allen, Texas 75002

Printed in the United States of America
ISBN 1-55924-480-1

1 2 3 4 5   94 93 92 91 90

CONTENTS

Search for Serenity and God in an Age of Stress

*Jesus said, "Let us go off . . .
to some place where we will be alone."*
MARK 6:31

One day a friend visited the artist Henri Matisse. The friend's nerves were frazzled and frayed. Matisse said to him, "André, you must find the artichokes in your life." Then he led his friend to a patch of artichokes in his garden. "Each morning," Matisse said, "after I have worked a while, I come here to be still and meditate. This simple ritual inspires me, relaxes me, and gives me a new perspective toward my work."

What Matisse found in his "patch of artichokes" is what millions of people in the 1990s are searching for: serenity and God in an age of stress. Touching on this search, *Time* magazine reports that "stress-reduction salons" are springing up in the United States and Japan. These salons are attracting not only "harried executives" but also "anxious teens."

This search for serenity and God (even by "anxious teens") inspired the author to introduce his Chicago high school seniors to a program of daily meditation. Each class ended with a ten-minute meditation exercise. The impact of this year-long program on the students was truly remarkable.

Prayer Paths is an attempt to share this program with a wider audience:

- adult individuals in a home or office setting,
- adult groups in an RCIA or parish setting,
- youth groups in a school or CCD setting.

How to Use *Prayer Paths*

The following instructions are for using *Prayer Paths* with groups. But with minimal adaptation they are for personal use as well.

First, it is strongly recommended that all meditation sessions take place *at the end* of a group or class meeting, rather than at the beginning of it.

Second, it is recommended that lights be turned off during the meditation. This helps give the room a restful, prayerful atmosphere.

Finally, members of the group should be encouraged to take a prayer posture that will be conducive to ten minutes of quiet reflection. Most people need to experiment a little to discover what posture works best for them.

First Session

Use the "Introductory Meditation" on pages 9–12 to introduce the *Prayer Paths* program. In reading this meditation to the group, observe two kinds of *pauses.*

The first kind of pause is designated by a centered rule between certain segments of the meditation. This pause should be about twenty seconds long to give the group time to carry out the instruction just given. For example, the pause between the first and the second paragraph of "Introductory Meditation 1" should be about twenty seconds to give the group time to settle into a meditation posture. If the group settles rather quickly, the pause following this initial instruction may be shortened. However, all other pauses designated by a centered rule should be given the full twenty seconds.

The second kind of pause is simply a pause between paragraphs. This pause should never be longer than five seconds. The exact length should be determined by what seems appropriate, given the meaning or context of the paragraph preceding the pause.

"Introductory Meditation 1" ends with this instruction to the group: "Now, for the remaining _____ minutes, just rest there ..." This is typical of how every meditation exercise ends. The amount of time remaining should be communicated to the group. Check your watch for this. The exact amount of time remaining is important, because it gives the group an idea of how much time remains for silent reflection. The period of silence should always run about three minutes.

Second Session

Use the "Introductory Meditation" on pages 13–15 for the second session. Follow the same procedure that you used in the first session.

All Subsequent Sessions

The regular meditation program begins with the third session. This—and all subsequent sessions—consists of three parts, of approximately the following durations:

- Preparation (3 minutes)
- Meditation Exercise (4 minutes)
- Silent Reflection (3 minutes)

1. Preparation. This part consists in reading (prayerfully and slowly) one of the three "Preparation for Meditation" options (see pages 17–21). The purpose of this part is to help the meditators release tension and get in touch with themselves. It lasts about three minutes.

The author used a different option each week. He found that using the same option for a week helped the meditators to get used to it, while switching options each week added variety.

2. Meditation Exercise. This part consists in reading (prayerfully and slowly) one of the sixty meditation exercises found in this book. The exercises are equally divided among five "paths" (these are explained in the chapter introductions):

- Natural Paths
- Scriptural Paths
- Autobiographical Paths
- Vicarial Paths
- Devotional Paths

The author did not follow the exercises in the order they appear in this book. That is, he did not begin with "Natural Paths," take the twelve meditation exercises there, and then move on to "Scriptural Paths." Rather, for variety's sake, he alternated the exercises according to the following schedule:

MONDAY: Natural Paths
TUESDAY: Scriptural Paths
WEDNESDAY: Autobiographical Paths
THURSDAY: Vicarial Paths
FRIDAY: Devotional Paths

3. Silent Reflection. This part consists in complete silence. It is the most important part of the ten-minute session. Its effectiveness hinges on the first two parts *and the movement of the Spirit.*

Two Final Points

The first point is this. Sometimes people ask, "What do you do when you finish the sixty exercises in this book?" The simplest answer is, "Repeat the exercises, starting again at the beginning." Repetition is not an obstacle to prayer. More often it is a help, especially in meditation exercises of this type.

This brings us to the second point. Sometimes it is desirable to have a special meditation for a special occasion. Here are some of those occasions and suggested meditation exercises for each.

Christmas Week

13 Census Official
14 The Shepherd
15 The Soldier

Healing Service

19 The Deaf-mute
21 The Lamp
48 The Healing

Holy Week

17 The Beggar
23 Crucifixion
51 Jesus Dream
59 The Cross

Penance Service

39 Piri
47 Retreat Confession
49 Convict's Prayer
59 The Cross

Easter Week

20 Sunrise
56 One Solitary Life

Death of a Person

53 Dresser Card

You are now ready to begin the adventure of searching for serenity and God in an age of stress.

Introductory Meditations

First Session *(See pages 2–3.)*

Take a comfortable position
and close your eyes.

The human body has three tension areas,
especially, that need to be relaxed.

The first is the forehead and the eyebrows.
They're closely linked with feelings of worry.
That's why we get wrinkles in the forehead.
When the forehead and eyebrows are relaxed,
it's almost impossible to feel worried.
So relax your forehead and eyebrows right now.

A second tension area is the jaw.
It's one of the most expressive
parts of the body.
We grit our teeth when we're angry.
We clench our jaw when we're determined.
When our jaw is tense, it's hard to relax.
So relax it right now.
Let it sag and hang limp.

A final tension area is the chest.
When we speak our mind

about something that's bothering us, we say,
"Now that I've got that off my chest,
I can breathe again."
A tense chest makes breathing difficult.
So relax your chest; let your shoulders sag.

Now, monitor your breathing.
Don't change it; just monitor it.

Concentrate on the flow of air
passing through your nostrils.

When do you feel the flow of air more—
when you inhale or when you exhale?

When is the flow of air warmer—
when you inhale or when you exhale?
Why?

Is the flow of air passing through one nostril
greater than the flow in the other nostril?

When I say "Begin,"
count the number of times you inhale
before I say "Stop."

Begin. (Pause for one minute.)

Stop.

Most people
take fourteen to eighteen breaths a minute.

If you took eight,
your breathing is nearly perfect.

Now, when I say "Begin,"
open your mouth wide and exhale.
When you've exhausted all the air you can,
purse your lips and blow.

Begin.

What happened?

You were able to expel even more air.
This shows
that you still had air left in your lungs.

Our lungs hold six pints of air.
People sitting at a desk
inhale about a pint of air.
This means that they use only five-sixths
of their lung capacity.
Experts say
that if we'd restore our lungs to full use,
we'd sleep better, feel better,
and have more energy.

Now, when I say "Begin,"
slow down and deepen your breathing
just a tiny bit.
Don't force it; do it gently.

Begin.

Now, listen to these words from the Bible.

God created the heavens
and stretched them out;
he fashioned the earth
and all that lives there;
he gave life and breath
to all its people.

Now, for the remaining ____ minutes,
just rest there,
realizing that your life and your *breath*
are signs of God's personal love for you.

Second Session *(See page 3.)*

Take a comfortable position;
close your eyes and relax your body.

———————

Begin
by releasing the tension in your forehead.

Now, move down to your jaw
and release the tension there.

Finally, move down to your chest
and release the tension there.

Now, imagine all this tension and worry
flowing out of your body.
Feel it flowing out
through your fingers and your toes,
like water through an open faucet.

———————

Feel your body becoming relaxed
and your mind becoming calm.

———————

Now, monitor your breathing.

Concentrate on the rhythmic flow of air
passing through your nostrils
as you inhale and exhale.

Notice the cooler air as you inhale,
and the warmer air as you exhale.

———————

When I say "Begin,"
count the number of times you inhale
before I say "Stop."

Begin. (Pause for one minute.)

Stop.

Recall that most people
take fourteen to eighteen breaths a minute.
If you took eight,
your breathing is nearly perfect.

Physically, breathing points to life.
As long as we breathe, we're alive.
When we stop breathing and can't be revived,
a doctor pronounces us dead.

But breathing does more than point to life.
Breathing also points to the Creator of life.
The Book of Genesis says:

The Lord God
took some soil from the ground
and formed a person out of it;
God breathed life-giving breath
into the person's nostrils
and the person began to live.
GENESIS 2:7 (slightly adapted)

Besides pointing to the Creator of life,
breathing points to the Holy Spirit within us.
Jesus said to his disciples:

"As the Father sent me,
so I send you."
Then he breathed on them and said,
"Receive the Holy Spirit."

JOHN 20:21-22

———————

Now, pray after me in silence:
God the Father,
Son,
and Holy Spirit,
you are closer to me
than my own breath.
May each breath I take deepen my awareness
of your presence within me.

———————

Now, for the remaining _____ minutes,
just rest there in the presence of God
as trustingly
as a child rests in the presence of its mother.

Preparation
for Meditation

Option 1 *(See page 4.)*

Take a comfortable position;
close your eyes and relax your body.

———————

Begin
by relaxing any tightness in your forehead.

Now, move down to your jaw
and relax any tightness there.

Finally, move down to your chest
and relax any tightness there.

Now, imagine all tension and worry
flowing out of your body.
Feel it flowing out
through your fingers and toes,
like water through an open faucet.

———————

Feel your body becoming relaxed
and your mind becoming calm.

———————

Now, monitor your breathing.

Concentrate on the rhythmic flow of air
passing through your nostrils
as you inhale and exhale.

Feel the cooler air as you inhale,
and the warmer air as you exhale.

When I say "Begin,"
count the number of times you exhale
before I say "Stop."

Begin. (Pause for one minute.)

Stop.

Now, just rest there, relaxed and peaceful,
as you imagine the following.

[Read one of the meditation exercises slowly and reflectively.]

Option 2 *(See page 4.)*

Take a comfortable position;
close your eyes and relax your body.

Begin
by relaxing any tightness in your forehead.

Now, move down to your jaw
and relax any tightness there.

Finally, move down to your chest
and relax any tightness there.

Now, focus your attention on your heart.

Become aware
of its rhythmic beat within you.

Feel the blood pulse through your body,
massaging it gently, and leaving it relaxed.

Now, focus your attention on your mind.

Become aware of its activity,
making it hard for you to feel calm.

Now, imagine all mental activity
slowing down gently,
leaving your mind peaceful and calm.

Now, just rest there, relaxed and peaceful,
as you imagine the following.

[Read one of the meditation exercises slowly and reflectively.]

Option 3 *(See page 4.)*

Take a comfortable position;
close your eyes and relax your body.

———————

Begin
by relaxing any tightness in your forehead.

Now, move down to your jaw
and relax any tightness there.

Finally, move down to your chest
and relax any tightness there.

Now, imagine all tension and worry
flowing out of your body.
Feel it flowing out
through your fingers and your toes,
like water through an open faucet.

———————

Feel your body becoming relaxed
and your mind becoming calm.

———————

Now, monitor the sensations of your body.
Become aware of:

your clothes and shoes—embracing your body,
the chair, floor, or wall—supporting your back.

Now, become aware of your hands—
holding one another or resting at your side,

the movement of your body—
rising and falling rhythmically as you breathe.

Now, just rest there, relaxed and peaceful,
as you imagine the following.

[Read one of the meditation exercises slowly and reflectively.]

Natural Paths

1 *"Ask for the ancient paths
and where the best road is.
Walk in it, and you will live in peace."*
                                    JEREMIAH 6:16

A path is something
that has been worn smooth by years of use.
It's a kind of "map on the ground,"
something to follow as we travel along.

A *prayer path* is something like that.
It, too, is a kind of map.
It's something to follow as we pray.
It's something to keep us from getting lost
or moving in circles.

In the pages ahead,
we will explore five prayer paths
that people use.
We will begin with the *natural* path.

A natural path is simply one
that uses something in nature,
like a beautiful desert landscape,
to raise the mind and the heart to God.
It is something
that uses the ordinary things of life
as ways to encounter God.

Summer Rain

1

It's late in the afternoon on a hot day.
You're all alone on a secluded beach.

You've just emerged from a swim
and lie down to dry off.

You feel so good, lying on the warm sand
with no worries in the world.

You think,
"This is what heaven must be like."

_____

Suddenly, a dark cloud appears in the sky.
A warm breeze stirs
and cool raindrops begin to fall.

Hear and see the raindrops fall on the water,
forming millions of little rings.

_____

Feel the raindrops fall on your body
and roll down your shoulders,
your arms, your legs.

_____

Smell and taste the raindrops
as they flow down your face
and collect on your lips,
trickling across them.

_____

Suddenly, a feeling of joy floods your soul.
You feel at peace
with everything and everyone.

You just lie there in the rain:
grateful that you are alive,
grateful that you are a human being,
grateful that God created you.

———————

As you lie there enjoying the rain,
these words from the Book of Psalms
come to mind:

O Lord, our Lord,
your greatness is seen in all the world! . . .
Who are we, that you think of us?
Who are we, that you care for us?
You have made us inferior only to yourself;
you have crowned us with glory and honor.

PSALM 8:1, 4–5 (slightly adapted)

———————

Now, for the remaining ____ minutes,
just lie there on the beach, enjoying the rain,
grateful that God created you and loves you.

Beach Campfire

2

Imagine you and some close friends
decide to camp out all night
on a deserted beach.
You arrive before dark, build a fire,
and watch the sun sink below the horizon.

Soon the moon comes up
and throws a shimmering silver carpet
across the quiet surface of the lake.
Overhead, millions of stars shine down on you.
It's a lovely night.

As you lie around the campfire
with your friends,
your conversation goes deeper
than spoken words.

There's a special feeling present
that allows you
to communicate with one another
without speaking.

So you simply lie there around the fire,
enjoying one another's presence.

As you lie there,
watching the fire reflect off the faces
of your friends,
these words of Scripture come to mind:

How wonderful it is,
how pleasant, for God's people
to live together in harmony!   PSALM 133:1

Suddenly, it occurs to you
that this is the way
that God intended people to live.

God intended them to live together
in harmony and love.

Now, for the remaining ____ minutes,
just lie there around the crackling fire,
alone with your thoughts,
surrounded by your friends.

Golf Course

3

It's a lovely winter night.
The snow is deep; the sky is clear
except for an occasional cloud.

You are walking home after a basketball game.
You have boots on, and not a breeze is stirring,
so you decide to take a shortcut
across a golf course.

Midway across the course,
you see a bunker next to a green.
Playfully, you let yourself fall backward
against the side of the bunker.
The heavy snow cushions your fall
and packs comfortably around you.

From your snowy nest, you look up at the sky.
Every inch of it is blanketed with bright stars.
You just lie there, marveling at the sight.

Then something strange happens.
Even though you are completely alone,
you don't feel lonely.
You feel a oneness with the universe,
even with those distant stars
shining down on you.

Suddenly, a strange thought strikes you:
Maybe someone on one of those stars—
at this very moment—is looking down on Earth,
just as you're looking up at the stars.

These words of the Book of Psalms come to mind:

Praise the Lord from heaven,
you that live in the heights above. . . .
Praise him, sun and moon;
praise him . . . snow and clouds. . . .
Praise him . . . all peoples. . . .
Praise the Lord!   PSALM 148:1, 3, 8, 11, 14

Now, for the remaining ＿＿ minutes,
just lie there,
feeling at one with the universe
and with the God who created it.

California Coast 4

Imagine
you are driving along the California seacoast.
It is the end of the day,
and the sun is a huge ball of orange fire
as it slips gently below the horizon.

Suddenly,
you come upon a stretch of deserted beach.
You pull off the road
and walk down a path to the beach.

Everything is silent
except for the rhythmic sound of the surf.

———————

You take off your shoes
and walk barefoot through the wet surf.
It feels so cool and refreshing.

———————

After a while
you walk over to a large rock.
You sit down and rest your head and back
against it.

As you sit there,
your thoughts turn to God,
who seems to be everywhere:

in the sea breeze
as it blows gently against your skin,
in the sun as it slowly sinks below the horizon,
in the surf as it rolls up onto the beach
and then back again into the ocean.

———————

These words of the Book of Psalms
come to your mind:

Lord . . .
you are all around me on every side. . . .
Where could I go to escape from you?
Where could I get away
from your presence? . . .

I could ask the darkness to hide me
or the light around me to turn into night,
but even darkness is not dark for you,
and the night is as bright as the day.
Darkness and light are the same to you.
                                    PSALM 139:1, 5, 7, 11–12

O God, how great you are!

Now, for the remaining _____ minutes,
just rest there alone with your thoughts,
listening to the surf
and watching the sun sink out of sight.

Journey Inward   5

Imagine you're waiting for an elevator
on the fifth floor of a building.

The elevator comes.
But this elevator is different
from other elevators.
It doesn't take you to the bottom of a building.
It takes you
to the bottom of your innermost self.

You enter the elevator.
The door closes and you begin to descend.

Imagine these are your feelings
as you move downward, floor by floor,
into your innermost being.

Fifth floor: A sense of wonder
                  fills your mind,
                  for you've
                  never been there before.

_____

Fourth floor: A sense of mystery
                  fills your imagination
                  as you consider
                  what you might find
                  in your innermost being.

_____

Third floor: A sense of excitement
                  fills your body
                  as you anticipate finding
                  something marvelous there.

_____

Second floor:	An exhilaration
	fills your whole being.
First floor:	The elevator slows down.
	The door opens.
	What you see makes you
	fall on your knees
	and bow to the ground.

———

You see what the prophet Isaiah saw
when he wrote:

I saw the Lord. . . .
Around him
flaming creatures were standing . . .
calling out to each other:
"Holy, holy, holy!
The Lord Almighty is holy!" ISAIAH 6:1–3

———

Now, for the remaining ____ minutes,
just remain on your knees,
filled with awe at the fact
that God dwells in your innermost being.

Beaver Dam

It's a beautiful Sunday afternoon.
You're jogging along a riverbank in a woods.
Everything is peaceful and beautiful.

The only sound,
beside your breathing and your footsteps,
is the singing of birds.

After a while
you stop to rest at an old beaver dam.
You sit with your back against a tree.

Sitting there all alone, you begin to notice
how quiet and peaceful everything is—
only the sound of water spilling over the dam.
You close your eyes and listen.

After listening to the water for a while,
you begin to wonder:
Where'd all this peace and beauty come from?
Why haven't I noticed it before?

Suddenly, it dawns on you.
This peace and beauty comes from God.
It's always been there.
The trouble is
you've never taken the time to notice it.

These words of Scripture come to mind:

Praise the Lord, my soul!
O Lord, my God, how great you are! . . .
You make springs flow in the valleys,
and rivers run between the hills. . . .
In the trees near by,
the birds make their nests and sing.
From the sky you send rain . . .
and the earth is filled with your blessings. . . .

Lord, you have made so many things!
How wisely you made them all! . . .
Praise the Lord, my soul!

PSALM 104:1, 10, 12–13, 24, 35

Now, for the remaining ____ minutes,
just sit there in God's presence,
enjoying the soothing sound of the water
as it falls across the beaver dam.

Summer Campout 7

It is a warm summer night.
You're camped out all alone,
high up on the side of a mountain.

The reason you're all alone
is because your camping partners
think a storm is coming
and have decided
to sleep inside a deserted cabin nearby.
But you've decided to remain outside.

As you lie there in your sleeping bag,
you look out across the valley
at the lights of a distant town.
It's a peaceful sight.

———————

Soon you grow tired from the hard day's climb
and fall asleep.
It feels so good.

———————

Suddenly, you awaken with a start.

Thunder and lightning are everywhere.
Strangely enough, however,
you're not afraid.
You feel protected by God.

———————

A few minutes later,
a heavy rain begins to fall.
But you don't join the others in the cabin.
You take shelter under an overhanging cliff.

There you sit, marveling at the storm,
especially the lightning and the thunder.

These words of Scripture come to mind:

How great is God's power. . . .
God lets the rain pour from the clouds
in showers. . . .

God sends the lightning across the sky,
from one end of the earth to the other.
Then the roar of God's voice is heard,
the majestic sound of thunder,
and all the while the lightning flashes. . . .

The glory of God fills us with awe.

JOB 36:22, 28; 37:3–4, 22 (slightly adapted)

Now, for the remaining _____ minutes,
just sit there and marvel at the storm,
realizing that compared to the glory of God
the lightning is but a tiny spark.

Mountain Night 8

Imagine you're vacationing all alone
in a cabin on a mountain.

It's two o'clock in the morning;
you can't sleep.
You get up and walk barefoot out-of-doors.

You feel the morning dew on your feet.
You feel the cool air on your bare skin.

You listen to the sound
of beetles and crickets
singing in the night.

You gaze at the sky
filled with millions of beautiful, bright stars.

Suddenly, you feel a oneness with
the dew on the grass,
the beetles and crickets singing about you,
the Milky Way arched above you,
the stars and the moon looking down upon you.

These words
of the Book of Psalms come to mind:

How clearly the sky reveals God's glory!
How plainly it shows what he has done!
Each day announces it to the following day;
each night repeats it to the next. . . .

May the glory of the Lord last forever! . . .
Praise the Lord, my soul!

Praise the Lord!   PSALM 19:1–2; 104:31, 35

Now, for the remaining _____ minutes,
just stand there, gazing at the sky,
spellbound at the thought of the God
who could make such a beautiful night.

Refreshing Swim

9

Imagine it's a hot summer day.
You're walking through a forest.

_____

Suddenly, you come to a large clearing.

A lawn, resembling a golf green,
covers the clearing like a rug.
In the center is a small lake.
It's so clear you can see fish in the water
and the sand on the bottom.

_____

You remove your clothes
and dive in for a swim.
The cool water refreshes your body.
It makes you feel great just to be alive.

As you swim in the clear water,
you feel a oneness with the fish around you—
and they seem to feel a oneness with you.

_____

After swimming for a while,
you emerge from the water
and lie down on the soft grass
to let the warm sun dry your wet body.

As it does,
you feel God's presence in the sun.
You feel God's love in its warmth.
You wish you could lie here forever and ever,
bathed in God's presence and love.

_____

For the first time,
you understand these words of Scripture:

The Lord is my shepherd. . . .
He lets me rest in fields of green grass
and leads me to quiet pools of fresh water.

He gives me new strength.
He guides me in the right paths,
as he has promised.

Even if I go through the deepest darkness,
I will not be afraid, Lord. . . .
I know that your goodness and love
will be with me all my life;
and your house will be my home
as long as I live.   PSALM 23

Now, for the remaining ____ minutes,
just lie there in the warm sun,
marveling at the thought
that God loves you more than you love yourself.

Lake Skate

10

It's a beautiful winter night,
just before Christmas.

You're ice-skating with a group of friends
on a small lagoon just off a large lake.

A fire is burning on the shore.
Everyone is sitting around it,
laughing and talking.

_____

Then you do something unusual.
Quietly, you leave your friends and the fire
and skate off into the darkness toward the lake.
It's as though someone out there on the lake
is calling you.

_____

The moon is bright,
and there's a thick layer of snow on the ice.

As you move farther out onto the lake,
everything grows quiet.

Except for the sound of your skates,
there is absolute silence.

_____

As you skate along,
your whole body begins to respond
gracefully and athletically
to the rhythm of your legs and arms.

It's a fantastic feeling.

_____

Then something remarkable happens.
You start cutting figures
and doing body flips on the ice
that you never knew you could do before.

It's the most extraordinary feeling
you've ever had.

———————————

Now, for the remaining ____ minutes,
enjoy doing things on skates
that you never did before.

———————————

If you feel inclined,
talk out loud to God while you skate.
Thank God
for this glorious moment you're enjoying.
For it was God
who called you away from your friends
so that the two of you
could be together
in the middle of the lake.

Body Flight

11

Imagine you're lying on your bed at home.
It's springtime,
and the window to your room is open.

Suddenly, something remarkable happens.
Your body becomes very light,
floats up from the bed,
and passes through the open window.

Once outside, it soars up into the sky,
like an eagle freed from a cage.

Feel the rush of excitement
as your body soars upward toward the sun.

Feel the rush of excitement
as your body dives downward toward the earth.

Burst into song
as your body swoops across the hills and fields
below you.

See the earth covered with grass and trees.
See cars and trucks moving over expressways.
See houses and barns looking like tiny toys.

Now,
as your body soars and dives about,
listen to this poem.
Try to experience it with all of your senses.

In fantastic flights of fantasy,
I've ridden the wind, painted rainbows,
and planted my flag on the moon.

In magical moments of revelry,
I've streaked across the sky,
tunneled through clouds,
and played tag with angels.

———————————

In mystical moments of ecstasy,
I've soared to heaven, leaped out of my skin,
and touched the face of God.

———————————

Now, for the remaining _____ minutes,
continue gliding and soaring,
wherever you wish,
in rhythm to your favorite piece of music.

Mountain Monk 12

Imagine
that you are sitting on a high mountain.
Far below,
at the foot of the mountain,
is a great city.
The sun is setting in the distance.
The sight brings great peace to your soul.

Soon darkness begins to fall.
The city is transformed into a sea of lights.
As you sit there, looking down at the city,
what are your feelings?

Soon you hear footsteps behind you.
You turn around
and recognize an old monk
who lives on the mountain.
He pauses at your side and says,

"If you go down into the city tonight,
you will find God."

Then, without explanation, he disappears.

Something tells you the monk is right.
You decide to go down into the city
to search for God.

As you descend the mountain,
three questions enter your mind.

Where should I look for God first?
Why should I look for God in this place?
How will I know when I have found God?

Jesus said,

"I was hungry and you fed me,
thirsty and you gave me a drink;
I was a stranger and you received me. . . .
Whenever you did this
for one of the least important
of these brothers [or sisters] of mine,
you did it for me!"   MATTHEW 25:35, 40

Now, for the remaining ____ minutes,
just rest there,
reflecting on these words of Jesus
and how they relate to the monk's words:
"If you go down into the city tonight,
you will find God."

Scriptural
Paths

2

*Your word is a lamp to guide me
and a light for my path.*

A *scriptural* path is simply one
that uses Scripture as a way
of raising the mind and the heart to God.

Take the gospel story
of the person born blind (John 9:1–7).

One way to use this story as a prayer path
is to make it come alive.
It is to transport ourselves back in time
to the actual gospel event.

It is to experience in our imagination
everything that happened,
as if we were actually present at the event.

It is to put ourselves
in the shoes of a bystander
who saw Jesus restore the blind person's sight.
It is to experience in our mind and our heart
what the bystander did.

Census Official 13

Imagine you are a Roman official
living in Rome two thousand years ago.

Your job is to direct the taking of the census
in the conquered nations of Caesar's empire.
It's an important job because it determines
the amount of taxes
these nations must pay to Rome.
At this particular moment,
you're in a tiny country called Judea.

A decree from Caesar Augustus
has already ordered all the citizens
to return to their ancestral towns
to register for the census.

One night you find yourself
supervising the census
in the small Judean town called Bethlehem.
You are tired, but before going to bed,
you decide to go for a walk outside the town.

As you walk alone in the dark,
you notice a light coming from a nearby cave
in the hillside.
You walk over and look inside.
What you see amazes you.

A young mother has just given birth.
Her young husband is with her.
He sees you, recognizes you
as the census director, and invites you in.

When you see the baby,
you instinctively kneel down.
It's the most beautiful child you've ever seen.

Saint Luke writes in his Gospel:

Emperor Augustus ordered a census to be taken
throughout the Roman Empire. . . .
Joseph went . . . to the town of Bethlehem. . . .
He went to register with Mary,
who was promised in marriage to him.
She was pregnant,
and while they were in Bethlehem,
the time came for her to have her baby.
She gave birth to her first son,
wrapped him in cloths and laid him in a manger—
there was no room for them to stay in the inn.

LUKE 2:1, 4-7

Now, for the remaining _____ minutes,
just kneel before the child, sensing that
one of the most important moments in history
is taking place before your very eyes.

The Shepherd

14

Imagine you are a shepherd
living two thousand years ago
in a village near Bethlehem in Judea.
One night you and two of your friends
are out in a field, sitting around a campfire,
keeping watch over your sheep.

You take turns putting sticks on the fire.
Sometimes you talk.
Sometimes you just sit there silently
in the warm glow of the fire,
watching it burn and listening to it crackle.
That's what you are doing now—
just enjoying the fire.

———————

Suddenly, something like a ball of fire
appears in the sky.
It's so bright
that you have to shield your eyes from it.
You become terribly frightened.
You've never seen anything like this before.

———————

Then from the midst of the ball of fire
comes a voice, saying,
"Do not be afraid!"
The voice is so peaceful
that it takes away all your fears.
Then the voice says:

"A baby has just been born in a cave
in nearby Bethlehem.
The baby is the promised Messiah
for whom Israel has been waiting."

At once, voices begin to sing.
It's the most beautiful sound you've ever heard.

Then,
as quickly as the light and the voices appeared,
they disappear.

Saint Luke writes in his Gospel:

When the angels
went away from them back into heaven,
the shepherds said to one another,
"Let's go to Bethlehem
and see this thing that has happened,
which the Lord has told us."
So they hurried off
and found Mary and Joseph
and saw the baby lying in the manger.
LUKE 2:15-16

Now, for the remaining ____ minutes,
just stand there silently, gazing at the infant,
wondering why God chose you,
a lowly shepherd, to be the first to visit God's Son.

The Soldier

15

Imagine you are a Roman soldier in Judea
about the time that Jesus was born.
You are part of an occupation army
whose job is to keep peace in that tiny nation.

One night you become homesick
for your family in Rome.
You go outside into the moonlight.
You walk across a field to a nearby hill
and climb the hill slowly.

When you reach the top of the hill,
you look up into the star-studded sky.

All of a sudden, something remarkable happens.
Off in the distance,
toward a small town called Bethlehem,
you see an unusual star rising in the sky.
As it rises, it grows brighter and brighter.

Then something more remarkable happens.
As you gaze at the star,
your homesickness disappears,
and a tremendous peace fills your soul—
a peace unlike anything
you've ever experienced in your life.

As you continue to gaze at the star,
you can't help but think
that the peace you are experiencing
has something to do with that star.

You wonder where the star came from
and what it means.

———————

Saint Matthew writes in his Gospel:

*When Jesus was born . . . magi from the east
arrived in Jerusalem, saying,
"Where is the newborn king of the Jews?
We saw his star at its rising. . . ."*

*[The chief priests and the scribes] said . . .
"In Bethlehem. . . ."
[The magi] set out. And behold,
the star that they had seen at its rising
preceded them, until it came and stopped
over the place where the child was.
They were overjoyed . . .
and on entering . . .
they saw the child with Mary his mother.*

MATTHEW 2:1-2, 5, 9-11 (NAB)*

———————

Now, for the remaining _____ minutes,
just remain standing there on the hilltop,
gazing at the star
and enjoying the peace it brings
to your restless heart.

———————

*All Scripture passages marked (NAB) are taken from *The New American
Bible with Revised New Testament*. Copyright © 1970, 1986 by the
Confraternity of Christian Doctrine.

The Storm 16

Imagine you are living at the time of Jesus.

One evening you are down at the Sea of Galilee
with Peter and several other Apostles.
You are sitting on the dock,
watching the sun go down.

Suddenly, Jesus walks out onto the dock
and says,
"Let us go across to the other side."

Peter invites you to go along.
Jesus smiles, and you know you are welcome.

As the boat reaches the center of the lake,
you miss Jesus.
You look around and see him in the back,
sound asleep.
He is clearly tired from a day of preaching.

Suddenly, a strong wind begins to blow.
It gets stronger and stronger.

Saint Mark describes what happened next:

*The waves began to spill over into the boat,
so that it was about to fill with water.
Jesus was in the back . . . sleeping. . . .
The disciples woke him up and said,
"Teacher,
don't you care that we are about to die?"*

*Jesus stood up and commanded the wind,
"Be quiet!" and he said to the waves, "Be still!"
The wind died down,
and there was a great calm.* MARK 4:37–39

_____

You stand there with the Apostles,
looking at the lake in complete amazement,
wondering what this means.

_____

Suddenly, you feel a hand on your shoulder.
You look around.
It is Jesus.

He looks into your eyes and says to you,
"Do you still have no faith?"

_____

Now, for the remaining _____ minutes,
just rest there
with the hand of Jesus on your shoulder,
wondering why Jesus said this to you.

The Beggar   17

There's a story called "The Other Wise Man."
It's about a fourth wise man, named Artaban,
who was supposed to go with the other three
to search for the newborn king of the Jews.

As you listen to this variation of the story,
put yourself in Artaban's shoes.
Try to experience everything he does.

*Artaban leaves his palace
with a pouch of precious gems for the new king.
On his way to join the other three wise men,
he meets a crippled mother and her sick child.
He stops to help them.
His act of kindness delays him just enough
to miss his rendezvous with the other three men.*

---

*Artaban continues on, trying to make up time.
But once again, he meets someone in need:
a widow and three children.
They have been evicted from their home.*

*Artaban uses one of his precious gems
to buy shelter and food for them.*

---

*Once again, he sets out.
But once again, he meets someone in need.*

*Artaban never does catch up with the others.
Worse yet, he eventually
gives away all of his precious gems.*

Years pass and Artaban grows old and feeble.
He ends up far from his homeland
in a city called Jerusalem.
There he survives as a beggar.

One day Artaban sees a criminal
being marched off to be crucified.
His heart skips a beat.

For some reason,
he feels very close to this unfortunate man.
He wants to help him but can't
because he is too old and feeble.

Artaban is brokenhearted.

As the victim approaches
the place where Artaban is standing,
he turns, looks at Artaban, and says,
"Don't be brokenhearted, Artaban;
you've been helping me all your life."

For the remaining ____ minutes,
just rest there,
experiencing how Artaban felt at that moment.

The Letter

Imagine you go to the mailbox one day
and find an unusual-looking letter
addressed to you.
It's unlike any letter you've ever seen.

You go to your room, slit open the envelope,
and pull out the letter.

You can't believe what you see.

Across the top of the letter,
these words are written in big gold letters:
"A letter from Jesus."

At first,
you think the letter is a promotional gimmick
from some TV evangelist,
soliciting money for his ministry.

But as you hold the letter in your hand,
your body begins to tingle,
and a strange feeling comes over you—
a feeling unlike anything
that you've ever experienced before.

With your body still tingling,
you begin to read the letter. It says:

*What I am about to say to you in this letter
I have already communicated to you
in the Gospel according to John.
But my special love for you compels me
to repeat the message in this unusual way.*

You turn the page over to the other side,
wondering what the message is.

The message reads:

"A branch cannot bear fruit by itself;
it can do so only if it remains in the vine.
In the same way you cannot bear fruit
unless you remain in me.

"I am the vine, and you are the branches.
Whoever remains in me . . .
will bear much fruit. . . .
Whoever does not remain in me
is thrown out like a branch and dries up."

JOHN 15:4–6

Now, for the remaining ____ minutes,
just rest there, asking yourself
what special significance this message holds
for you at this moment in your life.

The Deaf-mute 19

One day some people brought Jesus a man
who could hardly hear or speak.
They begged Jesus to heal him.
Saint Mark's Gospel
tells us what happened then:

Jesus took him off alone,
away from the crowd,
put his fingers in the man's ears,
spat, and touched the man's tongue.
Then Jesus looked up to heaven,
gave a deep groan, and said to the man,
"Ephphatha," which means, "Open up!"
At once the man was able to hear,
his speech impediment was removed,
and he began to talk without any trouble.

MARK 7:33–35

Now, consider how you are like the man
in that gospel story.

You'd like to speak to Jesus in prayer,
but you find it almost impossible.
You seem to have
a spiritual speech impediment.

Likewise,
you'd like to hear Jesus speak to you in prayer,
but, likewise, you find it almost impossible.
You seem to have
a spiritual hearing impediment.

Suddenly, you think to yourself,
"Why don't I ask Jesus

to take away my speech impediment
and my hearing impediment?
Why don't I ask Jesus to heal me,
as he did the deaf-mute in the Gospel?"

Then, before you can answer your own question,
Jesus appears.

———————

You try to speak to Jesus, but no words come.
So you point to your tongue and to your ears.
Jesus understands.

Then Jesus does something unusual.
Instead of touching your tongue and your ears,
he touches your heart.

Then, as quickly as he appeared, he disappears.

———————

Now, for the remaining _____ minutes,
just rest there, pondering what Jesus did
and what it might mean.

Sunrise   20

A fifteen-year-old high school student
describes a remarkable experience he had.
Imagine you are the student.
Try to experience exactly what the student did.
The student writes:

*It was Easter Sunday morning,
and I was returning home from my paper route.
I passed Saint Gall's Church
just as the sun was coming up.*

*I had no intention of going in for Mass,
because I was in the midst
of a teenage rejection of religion.*

---

*Then it happened!
I turned around just as the sun
struck the silver cross in front of the church.
I couldn't take my eyes off its fiery brightness.
I was overcome
by a sense of what the Apostles must have felt
two thousand years ago
on this very same morning.
This feeling moved me deeply.*

---

*An unseen force seemed to take hold of me
and lead me up the steps to the church.
I opened the door, went in, and knelt down.
For the first time in a long time,
I prayed.
For the first time
I understood what Easter was all about.*

_____

These words of Scripture come to mind:

O God . . .
you have rescued me . . .
and kept me from defeat. . . .
In the shadow of your wings
I find protection. . . .
Your constant love reaches the heavens;
your faithfulness touches the skies.

PSALM 56:12–13; 57:1, 10

_____

Now, for the remaining ____ minutes,
just rest there, trying to appreciate
how the Apostles must have felt
when they saw Jesus alive
on Easter Sunday morning.

69

The Lamp

21

Imagine your body is suspended in space
above a city like New York.

As you look down on the city,
imagine the thousands of people living there
who are filled with anger and hatred.

Imagine the thousands of people
who have little love for God or neighbor.

Now turn your attention back to yourself
floating above the city.

Focus on the rhythmic breathing of your body.
As you inhale,
imagine God's love flowing into your body
through the pores of your skin.

As this love flows into your body,
imagine that it becomes trapped inside you,
building up a store of love within you.

Imagine your body becoming a great lamp,
radiating love to the city below you.

Now, just rest there for a minute,
allowing God's love to build up inside you
and radiate love from you to the city below.

Now, in the remaining ____ minutes,
pick out a person you know
who seems to need God's love in a special way.

When you have picked out someone,
mentally visit that person.
Place both your hands on the person's head.

As you exhale,
imagine God's love flowing out from your body,
through your hands, into the other person.

Stay with the person
as long as you feel you are needed.

If time permits, move on to another person
who needs God's love.

The Farmer

22

Imagine you are living in the time of Jesus.
You are seated on a hillside in Galilee.
It's a beautiful spring day.
The sky is blue; the grass is green and soft.
Everywhere you look, you see people.
They've come to hear Jesus speak.

———————

Suddenly, Jesus stands up.
A hush falls across the crowd.
In a strong, captivating voice, Jesus says:

"One day
a farmer went out to plant seed in a field.
Some seed fell on a path bordering the field.
But the soil on the path was so hard
that the seed couldn't take root.

"That seed is like God's word
when it falls into the heart of a person
who doesn't want to hear the truth.

———————

"Other seed fell on poor, rocky soil.
The seed took root and sprouted.
But the tiny plants soon baked to death
from the heat of the sun.

"That seed is like God's word
when a person welcomes it, at first,
but abandons it
when trials or temptations come.

———————

"Other seed fell among thorn bushes
that bordered the field.
The seed took root and sprouted.
But the bushes choked the plants
before they could bear fruit.

"That seed is like God's word
when a person welcomes it, at first,
but gradually forgets about it
amid the daily activities of life.

"Finally, some seed fell on good soil.
It took root, grew, and bore much fruit.

"That seed is like God's word
when it falls into the heart of a person
who welcomes it and holds fast to it,
neither forgetting it in daily life
nor forgoing it in time of temptation."

LUKE 8:4-8, 11-15 (paraphrased)

Now, for the remaining _____ minutes,
imagine that when Jesus finishes speaking,
he walks over to you, sits down, and says,
"Tell me about your heart."

Crucifixion 23

Imagine you are in a time machine.
You are going back two thousand years
to the time of Jesus
and to the city of Jerusalem.

You arrive on Good Friday.
Within minutes, you find yourself on Calvary,
where Jesus is being crucified.

You want to rush up and stop this terrible thing.
You want to tell everybody
that you've just come
from the twentieth century
and what they're doing is wrong—
terribly wrong.
But you know they'd never understand.

So you just stand there,
beneath the cross of Jesus, filled with grief.

You want to pray, but you can't.
So you just stand there, looking at Jesus.

Suddenly,
Jesus looks upward into the sky.
Then he cries in a loud voice,
"Father! In your hands I place my spirit!"

A hush falls over the crowd.

In the midst of the eerie silence,
a Roman soldier, standing beside you, gasps,
"This man was really the Son of God!"

Minutes later,
you find yourself back in the time machine.
You're returning to the twentieth century.

As you sit there,
grief-stricken by what you've seen,
you ask yourself three questions:

What have I done for Jesus so far in my life?
What am I doing for him right now?
What ought I to do for him in the future?

_____

Now, for the remaining ____ minutes,
just sit there,
pondering those three questions:

What have I done for Jesus so far in my life?
What am I doing for him right now?
What ought I to do for him in the future?

World's End 24

You are vacationing alone in a mountain cabin
miles from all civilization.
You don't have a telephone in the cabin,
but you do have a television set.
One night, about midnight,
you are watching a movie.
Suddenly, the movie is interrupted
by a special news bulletin.

The bulletin says
that astronomers at the national observatory
have reported shocking news:
a mysterious planet of immense magnitude
has broken from its orbit
and is plunging toward earth
at an incredible, accelerating rate of speed.

The astronomers estimate
that the mystery planet will collide with earth
in less than an hour.

They say
that the collision will cause an explosion
that will disintegrate both planets.
Finally, they say
that as the planet approaches earth
it will disrupt television communication,
leaving all television screens blank.

After the announcement, the television camera
cuts away to the mysterious planet.

It shows the planet streaking toward earth,
getting brighter and brighter as it approaches.

As you watch the approaching planet,
you hear these words come from the set:
"The president of the United States
would like to make a brief statement."

Then, in an emotional voice,
you hear the president say:

"My fellow Americans,
I urge you to embrace one another in love
and to pray to God."

Before the president can say another word,
the TV screen goes blank
and the set goes silent.
The approaching planet has disrupted
all further television communication.

Now, for the remaining ____ minutes,
just remain there in your mountain cabin alone,
awaiting the end.

Autobiographical
Paths

3 *Lord . . . you know my path.*

PSALM 142:2, 4 (NAB)

Saint Augustine wrote:

We stand in wonder
at towering mountains,
crashing waves,
and orbiting stars;
but forget to wonder at ourselves.

Saint Augustine was alluding to the fact
that one of the best *prayer paths* to God
is one that is often least traveled.
It is the *autobiographical* path.

An autobiographical prayer path is simply one
that uses the episodes and experiences
of our own lives
to raise our mind and our heart to God.

It is one
that uses our innermost dreams and doubts
as ways to encounter God.

Best Friend 25

Call to mind your best friend,
or someone you like very much.

_____

Now recall the first time you realized
that you liked this person in a special way.

_____

What are some of the things
that you like about this person?

_____

Now recall one of the most pleasant times
that you've had with this person.

_____

If you could choose a week's vacation
with this person,
where would you like to go,
and what would you like to do?

_____

Now listen to these words of Scripture:

_Jonathan was deeply attracted to David
and came to love him
as much as he loved himself. . . ._

_Jonathan swore an eternal friendship with David
because of his deep affection for him.
He took off the robe he was wearing
and gave it to David,
together with his armor and also his sword._

1 SAMUEL 18:1, 3–4

Now, for the remaining _____ minutes,
just rest there,
marveling at a tremendous mystery.
It is this.

Jesus Christ, the Son of God,
loves you infinitely more
than you love the person
you have just been thinking about.

Good Things

26

Imagine that you're able to step *outside*
your own body
and see yourself through your own eyes.

What's one thing about yourself
that you really like?

_____

Now imagine that you're able to step *inside*
the body of a family member
with whom you get along fairly well.
See yourself through that person's eyes.

What's one thing
he or she seems to like about you?

_____

Now imagine
that you are able to step inside the body
of a fairly close friend
and see yourself through his or her eyes.

What's one thing
that friend seems to like about you?

_____

Are the things
that you and others like about you
mainly *God-given?*
That is, are they things
related to your body or your talents?

Or are they things
that are mainly *family-given?*
That is, are they things
related to your home life, like having

supportive parents, good brothers or sisters,
or financial security?

Or are they things
that are mainly *self-acquired?*
That is, are they things
you've acquired by discipline and hard work,
like faithful friends
or academic, athletic, or business success?

Now, in the remaining ____ minutes,
focus on one thing
that you or others like about you.

Consider how you might use that one thing
in such a way
that you'll be proud when you stand before God
at the end of your life.

Bad Things

27

Imagine that you're able to step *outside*
your own body
and see yourself through your own eyes.

What's one thing
that you see in yourself that you dislike?

_____

Now imagine that you're able to step *inside*
the body of a family member
with whom you get along the least.
See yourself through that person's eyes.

What's one thing
that he or she seems to dislike about you?

_____

Now imagine
that you're able to step inside the body
of someone who doesn't seem to like you.
See yourself through that person's eyes.
What's one thing
that he or she seems to dislike about you?

_____

Are the things that you and others dislike
mainly *God-given?*
That is, are they things
related to your body or your talents?

Or are they things
that are mainly *family-given?*
That is, are they things
related to your home life,
like divorce, alcoholism, or financial problems?

Or are they things
that are mainly *self-acquired?*
That is, are they things
that you're responsible for,
like laziness, selfishness, or jealousy?

—————————

Now, in the remaining ____ minutes,
focus on one thing
that you or others dislike about you.

Consider what you might do about it
so that it will become less of a problem
for you or for others.

If you feel comfortable doing so,
ask Jesus what he would advise you to do
about this one thing.

Life Replay

28

Go back to last summer.
Recall a pleasant experience that you had.

Spend just a minute or so
replaying the experience
and enjoying it all over again.

Now go back in time
to a summer when you were in grade school.

Do the same thing.
Recall a pleasant experience that you had.
Replay it and enjoy it all over again.

Now go back in time to your earliest childhood.

Again, do the same thing.
Pick out a pleasant experience and replay it.

Now go back
to the week before you were born.

Imagine the joy your parents felt
as they awaited your birth.

Now listen to these words of God,
inspired by the Book of Psalms:

I created every part of you,
put you together in your mother's womb. . . .
When you were there, growing in secret,
I loved you.

I loved you with an infinite love then;
and I still do now.   Inspired by PSALM 139:13, 15

Now, for the remaining _____ minutes,
rest there in God's presence,
realizing that in spite of all your shortcomings,
God loves you with an infinite love.

One Change

29

If you could change one thing in your life,
what would it be?

_____

Is this one thing
something over which you have *total* control,
like simply swallowing your pride
and seeking help
in dealing with some personal problem?

_____

Or is it something
over which you have only *partial* control,
like working harder and longer
to try to win a job or a position,
knowing that in the end
another person has the power
to give it to you or not?

_____

Or is it something
over which you have *no* control at all,
like a divorce or a serious family problem?

_____

Now imagine that your best friend
wanted to change this very same thing
in his or her life.
What advice would you give your friend
concerning it?

_____

Now, for the remaining _____ minutes,
just rest there,
considering the one thing
that you would like to change in your life.

If you feel moved to do so,
speak to Jesus about it.

Ask him what advice he would give you
concerning it.

Retreat Sharing

30

Imagine
you're on a retreat with about forty people.

On the second night,
the director breaks the large group
into smaller groups of four people each.
To your delight,
the other three people in your group
are your closest friends.

Who would these three people be?

———————

The director instructs each person in the group
to share with the other three
the following:
one disappointment from your past,
one difficulty you're having right now,
and one wild dream concerning the future.

As each of your three friends shares,
you're amazed
at how honest and personal they are.

Now your turn comes.
Because of the example of your three friends,
you open yourself totally to them.

First, you share with them
a disappointment from the past.
What would that disappointment be?

———————

Next, you share with them a difficulty
you're having in the present.
What is it?

Finally, you share with them a dream
you'd love to have come true in your future.
What would that dream be?

After sharing with your friends,
you feel closer to them than you've ever felt.
And it's obvious
that they feel the same way about you.

Spontaneously, the four of you huddle together,
bow your heads,
and pray silently for one another.

Now, for the remaining ____ minutes,
think of each friend individually
and do two things:
Tell God what you like about that person,
and make a prayer to God for him or her.

The Store

31

Imagine it is two o'clock in the morning.
You have been startled from your sleep
by an unusual dream.

You dreamed
that you were walking through a store.

Instead of selling things
that you put *on* yourself—
like shoes, shirts, pants—
this store sells things
that you put *inside* yourself—
like a better personality, greater faith in God,
a more positive attitude toward others,
a greater enthusiasm for life.

After looking around for a while,
you see something you really want
and decide to buy it, regardless of the price.

What did you choose to buy?

_____

Why did you choose to buy this item?
How can it help you in a special way
at this time in your life?

_____

When you go to pay for the item,
the cashier tells you
that you can't pay for it all at once,
and that you can't pay for it with money.

You can only buy it on an installment plan
that requires you to pay a certain amount
every day for the rest of your life.
And the way you are to pay for it

is by voluntarily
spending a certain amount of time each day
doing something for others,
especially those who are in no position
to return the favor or reward you for it.

———————

The cashier then asks you
how many minutes a day you would be willing
to spend doing this
to buy the item that you have just chosen.

What do you answer?

———————

Now suppose the cashier told you
that your offer was not enough.
How much higher would you go
before deciding the price was too high?

———————

For the remaining ____ minutes,
reflect upon the dream
and what meaning it might contain for you.

Last Day

32

A group of college students
were given this assignment.

"Imagine that you have a rare disease.
You feel fine,
but the doctor says
that you have only twenty-four hours to live.
How will you spend those twenty-four hours?"

———————

Here's what one girl wrote:

If I had only a short time to live,
I would immediately contact all the people
I had ever really loved,
and I'd make sure they knew
I had really loved them.

Then I would play all the records
that meant the most to me,
and I would sing all my favorite songs.
And oh, I would dance.
I would dance all night. . . .

Then I would thank God
for the great gift of life, and die in his arms.

———————

Now imagine
that you have only twenty-four hours to live.
How will you spend these final hours?
How much time will you spend alone?
How much time with people?

———————

Apart from your family,
what two people
will you make a special effort to see?
What will you talk about with them?

_____

Now imagine yourself at your own funeral.
See your family seated in the front row.
See your closest friends seated behind them.

Hear the music.
Smell the flowers and the burning candles.
Listen to what the homilist says about you.

_____

Now, for the remaining _____ minutes,
imagine that you decided
to record a four- or five-line *spiritual* message
to be played back to your family and friends
at the end of the homily at your own funeral.
Note that it's a *spiritual* message—
not a *thank-you* or *I-love-you* message.

What message would you choose to give them?

Day Replay

33

Think back
over the past twenty-four hours.

What stands out *most* in your mind
about those twenty-four hours?

———————

Pick out one *good* thing
that happened to you during that period.
In other words, pick out one thing
that made you especially happy or glad.

———————

Now, relive the event you picked out.
Reexperience it in your imagination.
Conclude by talking to God about it.

———————

Now,
replay the past twenty-four hours again.

This time pick out one *bad* thing
that happened to you during that time.
In other words, pick out one thing
that you wish had *not* happened to you.

———————

Now, relive the event you picked out.
Reexperience it in your imagination.
Conclude by talking to God about it.

———————

Now, for the remaining ____ minutes,
reflect on each of these two things.

Ask yourself this question.
How will I probably feel about these things
when I remember them ten years from now?

Why will you probably feel this way
at that time?

Stalled Car

34

A high school student describes an episode
that took place during summer vacation.
As you listen to the description,
try to experience in your imagination
everything the student did.
The student writes:

Last summer
I was driving home on the expressway.
I came upon a stalled car
parked on the shoulder of the road.
A man and his family
were trying to flag down someone to help.
Nobody stopped.

I got off at the next exit,
drove back to the closest entrance ramp,
and got back onto the expressway.

On my second pass,
the man and his family were still there.

I pulled off the expressway
and stopped behind the stalled car.
It was a family of five:
a father, a mother, and three small children.

The man explained his problem to me.
Then all five got into my car,
and I drove them to the nearest gas station.

---

*I couldn't believe how genuinely grateful
the family was for the help I gave them.*

*Later that day,
I couldn't believe something else:
the joy I felt because I had helped the family.
That experience made me want to do
more things for more people.*

Now, in the remaining _____ minutes,
try to experience what it was
that made the student go to all the trouble
of leaving the expressway
and returning again to help the family.

Recall a time
when you did something similar for someone.

The Child

35

It's about three o'clock in the morning.
You've just awakened from a strange dream.
In the dream you were walking through a park.

As you walked along,
you suddenly noticed a child following you.
At first you thought nothing of it.
But when the child continued to follow you
after you left the park, you became concerned.

After walking about a block,
you stopped, turned around,
and said to the child, "Can I help you?"

The child stared at you, as if you were a ghost.

Then something amazing happened.
You suddenly recognized who the child was.
It was yourself at the age of six.

After a minute, the shock wore off a bit,
and you regained your composure.

You said to the child,
"Are you real, or am I imagining all of this?"

The child smiled and said,
"I'm real, all right.
I have a message from God."

Now you're thrown back into shock.
Why was God sending you a message
through the child you used to be?

After a minute, the child said,
"God wants to know if you are happy
with the way things have turned out for you.
Or would you like to start over again
at age six?"

Now, for the remaining ____ minutes,
do two things.

First, identify one thing in your life
that you're happy about
and wouldn't want to change
if God asked you to start your life over again.

Second, identify one thing in your life
that you're not too happy about
and would change
if God told you to start over again.

One Problem

36

Pick out one problem
that's bothering you right now, for example,
a relationship with someone
that's not going too well,
or a family situation
that's disturbing your peace of mind.

_____

On a scale of one to ten,
rate how responsible you are for the problem—
one being not responsible at all,
ten being totally responsible.

_____

If you gave yourself a rating of three or better,
why did you do so?
In other words,
how are you partially to blame for the problem?

_____

Regardless of who is to blame,
what is *one thing* you could do
to lessen the problem—
or to lessen the impact
it's having on your peace of mind?

_____

What keeps you from doing this one thing
to improve the situation?

_____

Now, for the remaining ____ minutes,
consider

what you would advise your best friend to do
if he or she had your problem
and asked your advice on how to handle it.

Or if you feel comfortable in doing so,
ask Jesus how he might handle your problem
if he were in your shoes.

Vicarial Paths

4 *Walk in the way of good people,*
and keep to the paths of the just.

PROVERBS 2:20 (NAB, slightly adapted)

A direct experience
is an experience that happens to us.
It is a firsthand experience.

An indirect experience
is one that happens to another person,
but which we share
by putting ourselves in that person's shoes.

In other words,
we experience in our imagination
what happened to the other person.
Such an experience is also called
a vicarious experience.

A *vicarial* prayer path, therefore,
is simply one
that uses another's experience
to raise our own mind and heart to God.
It is reliving another's experience
and using it
as a way to encounter God in prayer.

Sky Dive

37

Seventeen-year-old Mike Valentino
describes his first sky dive.
As you listen to his description,
experience in your imagination
everything that he does. He writes:

Our single-engine Cessna takes off smoothly.
It climbs effortlessly to the assigned altitude.
The sky is beautiful,
and I pray that it will accept me.

My jump-master opens the door slightly.
A ninety-mile-an-hour wind hits my face.
I love it!

———————

The pilot cuts the engine of the plane.
I stare down at the ground—
twenty-eight-hundred feet below me.

———————

My jump-master pats me on the back.
I hesitate a second to erase all doubts.
I jump!

For a split second I feel I'm falling wrong.
For a split second I fear something's not right.
I stretch! I battle the wind.
I strive to become like a badminton bird:
body arched, belly pointed downward,
arms and legs upstretched like feathers.

Then, suddenly, I make it!
Now I am like a bird; I am poetry in motion.
Tears are in my eyes—tears of joy.
I scream: "Thank you, God!"

_____

It's silent up here—
like the inside of a vast cathedral.
I can hear myself breathe.
I can hear my heart beat.

_____

It's a special place here—God's place—
and more beautiful than I ever dreamed.

It's a heaven here!
Yes, a heaven!

I feel as if I'm dreaming,
yet no dream was ever so real.

_____

Now, for the remaining ____ minutes,
listen to yourself breathe
and feel your heart beat,
experiencing in your imagination
the joy and excitement that Mike did.

Highway Accident

38

One night,
when he was still in college,
Keith Miller was badly hurt in a car accident
on a deserted road.
As he lay there waiting for help, he prayed.

He said later that as he prayed,
a deep peace came over him
and for the first time in his life
he wasn't afraid to die.

Now imagine that you're a college student.
You're driving home down a deserted road
about one o'clock in the morning.

Suddenly, you lose control of your car.
It goes off the road and turns over.
You're thrown out of the car
and are badly hurt.

You lie on the side of the road,
fearing that you'll die before anyone finds you.

After about ten minutes,
you hear a car approaching.
The driver spots you and stops.
Sensing the gravity of your condition,
she tells you to lie perfectly still
until she can get an ambulance.

She warns you, however,
that there are no large towns nearby.
It might be an hour
before the ambulance arrives.

110

She drives off.
You lie there all alone in the darkness,
afraid that you will die
before help comes.

What are your thoughts?

After a while, you begin to pray.
As you do, something incredible happens.

A feeling of deep peace comes over you,
and you're no longer afraid that you'll die.

About thirty minutes later,
an ambulance comes
and takes you to a hospital.
You eventually recuperate.

Months later, you recall the accident.
You ask yourself,
Why did my fear of death vanish and
a deep peace come over me after I prayed?

Now, for the remaining ____ minutes,
think about
what God was trying to teach you
that night by the side of the road.

Piri

39

Piri Thomas
was a drug pusher and an attempted killer.
Now listen to a retelling of Piri's story.
As you do, try to experience everything he did.

One night
Piri was in prison lying on his cell bunk.
He was thinking about the tragic direction
that his young life had taken.

Suddenly, Piri felt the urge to do something
that he hadn't done since childhood.

He felt the urge to pray.

So he waited until he was sure
that his cell mate was fast asleep.
Then he climbed down from his bunk,
knelt on the cold cell floor,
and prayed aloud.

He talked to God
as if God were right there in the cell with him.
He talked to God honestly and from the heart
for about five minutes.

Finally, Piri ended his prayer with an "Amen."

Then something happened that startled Piri.
Out of the darkness came another "Amen."
It was the voice of his young cell mate.

The two prisoners talked long into the night.
They shared with one another
things they had not shared with anyone else.

---

*Finally, Piri said, "Good night, Chico.
I'm thinking that God is always with us.
It's just that we are not always with God."*

---

*Just as Piri was dropping off to sleep,
he heard young Chico crying.
"Cry, Chico," he said to himself,
"I hear even Christ cried."*

Now, for the remaining _____ minutes,
just rest there.
If you can do so, do what Piri did.
Talk to God about your life—
honestly and from the heart.

Driftwood

40

Imagine you are the student
who wrote the following.
In your imagination, relive the experience,
just as the student describes it.

Last Saturday,
about ten of us went up to my family's cottage
on Lake Michigan.
It was a cool day,
so we went to the beach fairly well clothed.

Toward the end of the afternoon,
we built a fire and watched the sun set.

At one point,
I could almost feel the friendship
that we had for one another.

The next day I learned that one of my friends
had left some clothes at the cottage.
So I drove back by myself.
I enjoyed the ride because of the peacefulness
and because of the beautiful autumn colors.

When I got to the cottage, I ate lunch.
Then I went down to the beach.
I walked for about a mile,
just looking at the water
and thinking about the day before.
I could almost hear the voices of my friends,
lingering in the air, like spirits.

I stopped at the place
where we had built our fire.

There I found a piece of driftwood
on which one of the girls
had carved all of our initials.
A special joy filled my heart.
I picked up the driftwood and brought it home.

Later, I gave it to the girl
to keep for all of us
as a remembrance of a beautiful day.

For the remaining ＿＿ minutes,
recall a similar experience
that you had with some friends.
Try to recapture the experience
in all its details,
just as the high school student did.

Canoe Trip

41

Imagine you are the high school student
who describes this experience. She writes:

*I will never forget a canoe trip
that I made with some of my friends.
We had been looking forward to it all summer
and were in a great mood.
As we got into the canoe,
everyone was laughing and talking.
It promised to be
the greatest day of the summer.*

———————

*About two hours into our trip down the river,
the sky turned black and it began to pour rain.*

*It didn't take long for all of us
to become soaked, cold, and miserable.*

*The trip
that we had been looking forward to for so long
was turning into a disaster.*

———————

*Suddenly,
one of my friends stood up in the canoe
and sang "Singin' in the Rain."*

*He got so involved in his song
that he tipped over the canoe,
and we all went flying into the river.*

———————

*My friend kept right on singing in the water,
and we all came up laughing.*

We got back into the canoe
and continued down the river,
laughing, splashing, and singing in the rain—
having more fun
than we ever imagined possible.

That day, singing in the pouring rain,
I discovered something I'll never forget.
We all have within ourselves
the power to change a bad situation
into a fantastic experience.

Saint Paul writes:
"Do not let evil defeat you;
instead, conquer evil with good." ROMANS 12:21

Now, for the remaining _____ minutes,
float down the river with your friends,
singing in the rain
and realizing that thanks to Jesus Christ,
nothing can defeat you, not even evil.

Death   42

Imagine you are the person in this story.
Experience everything the person does.
See what the person sees;
hear what the person hears;
feel what the person feels.

A merchant in ancient Baghdad
sent a servant to the marketplace
to buy some provisions.
Shortly afterward, the servant returned,
pale and trembling from head to foot.

The merchant said to the servant,
"What is wrong?
You look terrible!"

"Master! Master!" cried the servant.
"Just a few minutes ago in the marketplace,
I was jostled rudely by a man in the crowd.
When I turned to see who would do such a thing,
I saw it was Death.
And Death glared at me in a threatening way,
as if I were its next victim."

Then the servant said to the merchant,
"Please lend me your fastest horse
that I may flee to far-off Samarra.
Death will never think of looking for me there."

The merchant gladly lent the servant
the fastest horse.
The servant mounted, galloped off,
and disappeared over the horizon.

―――――――――――――――――――

―――――――――

After the servant had gone,
the merchant went to the marketplace
to buy the provisions
that the servant had failed to get.
When the merchant got there,
lo and behold,
who should be there but Death.

―――――――――

The merchant went up to Death and said,
"Why did you glare at my servant this morning
in such a threatening way?"

"That was not a threatening look," said Death.
"It was a look of surprise.
I was surprised to see your servant in Baghdad,
for I had an appointment
with your servant tonight in far-off Samarra."

Paraphrased from a story by Somerset Maugham

―――――――――

Now, for the remaining ＿＿ minutes,
just remain there,
pondering the meaning of the story
and what message
it might hold for you, personally.

120

Mountain Blizzard 43

One December day,
sixteen-year-old Gary Schneider
and two friends
set out on a four-day climb up Mount Hood.
As you listen to this retelling of their story,
try to experience everything they did.

On the second day of the climb,
a raging blizzard struck.
Unable to move up or down the mountain,
the boys tunneled into a snowbank
to wait out the snowstorm.

A week passed, and the blizzard raged on.
The boys passed the time
reading from a small pocket Bible
that Gary had stashed in his climbing gear.

The only light they had
was the spooky reflected light
of the snow tunnel leading into their snow cave.

It was an eerie sight:
one boy lying in his sleeping bag reading,
the other two, in their sleeping bags, listening.
Periodically, they paused to pray,
sometimes out loud together,
sometimes alone in silence.

As the blizzard entered the second week,
the boys were down to a ration of food
of two spoonfuls of pancake batter a day.

*Their only source of hope and strength
was the Bible.
Psalm 130 described their situation perfectly:*

*"From the depths of our despair
we call to you, Lord.
We trust in your word.
We wait for you to help us
more eagerly than night watchmen
wait for the dawn."* PSALM 130:1, 5-6 (slightly adapted)

―――――――――

*Finally, on the sixteenth day,
the weather cleared.
The boys emerged from their snow cave.
Weakened badly, they could hardly walk.*

*Then they spotted a rescue team.
Their ordeal was over.*

―――――――――

Now, for the remaining ＿＿ minutes,
just rest there,
trying to imagine how the boys must have felt
when the blizzard was still raging
and they were practically out of food,
and when the blizzard stopped
and they spotted the rescue team.

Glenn's Dream

44

When Glenn Cunningham was seven years old,
his legs were so badly burned
that doctors considered amputation.
At the last minute,
they decided against it.
They told Glenn, however,
that he'd probably never stand or walk again.

When the burns on Glenn's legs began to heal,
he set out to prove the doctors wrong.

First, Glenn stood.
Then, he walked.
Then came the day when he ran.
He didn't run fast, but he ran.

Now
Glenn began to exercise his legs vigorously.
He worked hard.
He worked long.
He never stopped working.
He was a teenager with a dream.

Eventually, Glenn went to college.
His extracurricular activity was track.
No longer
was he running to prove doctors wrong.
He was now running because he was good at it.

Soon college records
began to fall under his driving legs.

Then came the Berlin Olympics.
Glenn not only ran in them
but also broke the Olympic record
for the 1,500 meter race.

The following year,
Glenn broke the world's indoor mile record.

The boy who wasn't supposed to stand or walk
became the world's fastest human being.

Jesus said,
"Ask, and you will receive;
seek, and you will find;
knock, and the door will be opened to you."
MATTHEW 7:7

Now, for the remaining _____ minutes,
just rest there,
realizing you can make any dream come true—
if you work hard enough,
long enough,
and never stop dreaming.

Trapper's Cabin

45

Two high school students were vacationing
alone in the Canadian wilderness.

They had been canoeing for about a week
and were tired and in need of rest.
Suddenly, they spotted a trapper's cabin.
They beached their canoe, went up to the cabin,
and tried the door cautiously. It was open.

The cabin was empty except for a cot.
On the cot lay an open Bible.
Across the pages of the Bible lay a note.
It turned out to be from someone who,
like themselves,
had been canoeing in the wilderness,
had taken sick, found the open cabin,
and used it. The note read:

I had taken seriously ill and needed shelter.
Your cabin provided it.
I cannot repay you with money,
only with God's promise in the Bible.
Read the passage below this note.

The boys lifted the note,
wondering what the passage said.

The Bible passage was a description
of the Last Judgment. It said:

"Then the King will say
to the people on his right,
'Come, you that are blessed by my Father! . . .
I was a stranger

and you received me in your homes . . .
I was sick, and you took care of me. . . .'

"The righteous will then answer him . . .
'When did we ever see you a stranger
and welcome you in our homes, or . . .
sick [and take care of you]?'

"The King will reply,
'I tell you, whenever you did this
for one of the least important
of these brothers [and sisters] of mine,
you did it for me!' "   MATTHEW 25:34–40

Later, one of the boys said,
"I'd read that Bible passage many times,
but never before did it mean so much to me
as it did at that moment in the trapper's cabin."

Now, for the remaining ____ minutes,
just rest there,
trying to realize this incredible truth:
When you help someone in need,
you help Jesus himself.

Father's Letter

46

In his earlier years, Jimmy Stewart
was one of Hollywood's most respected actors.
When World War II broke out,
he enlisted as a pilot.

Before he left for Europe,
his dad embraced him affectionately.
For a long while they held each other close.

Only later did Jimmy discover
that while they were embracing,
his dad slipped an envelope into his pocket.
Later that night, Jimmy found it.
For a while he just held it lovingly,
wondering what was in it.

Finally, Jimmy opened it.
The letter said:

My dear Jim boy,
Soon after you read this letter,
you will be on your way
to the worst sort of danger. . . .
I am banking on the enclosed copy
of the 91st Psalm.
The thing that takes the place of fear
and worry is the promise of these words. . . .
I can say no more. . . .
I love you more than I can tell you.

Dad

Jimmy brushed away the tears from his eyes
and read these words from Psalm 91:

You will be safe in [God's] care;
his faithfulness will protect and defend you.
You need not fear. . . .
God will put his angels in charge of you
to protect you wherever you go.

PSALM 91:4–5, 11

Now, for the remaining ____ minutes,
think back over your own life
and recall something especially loving
that your father or mother did for you
on some special occasion.

Retreat Confession

47

John Egan was making a high school retreat.
On the last day, he decided
to do something that he'd been putting off.
He decided to go to confession—
holding nothing back, but telling it all
as honestly and frankly as he could.

———————

To John's surprise,
the priest didn't speak to him about his sins.
He spoke to him
only about God's great love for him.

———————

Now, put yourself in John's shoes
as you listen
to what happened to him after his confession.
Try to experience what he did.
John writes:

*I left the chapel enormously relieved and
walked out into the beauty of the afternoon. . . .
I became acutely aware of the glory
of that April day. . . .*

*Joy began to well up and run in my heart . . .
growing and surging . . .
different from anything
that I'd ever experienced before . . .
purer and richer.*

*As I walked alone,
stunned by the newness of it all . . .
that pure, rich joy grew and expanded. . . .
I don't think I'd ever been happier
in my life. . . .*

I wandered along . . .
not knowing or caring where my feet went. . . .
At length
I found myself way out on the golf course.
I remember lying down out of sheer joy
on a bunker
with my eyes to the blue sky
and my arms wide open to the Lord. . . .

How long I lay there I don't remember.
All I do remember is
that I felt enormously close to God.*

Now, for the remaining _____ minutes,
just lie there on the bunker
with your arms outstretched,
looking up into the blue sky,
feeling enormously close to God.

*Slightly adapted from *A Traveller Toward the Dawn: The Spiritual Journal of John Egan, S.J.*, edited by William J. O'Malley, S.J. (Chicago: Loyola University Press, 1990), pp. 6–7. Used by permission.

The Healing

48

Imagine you are the young person
who wrote the following.
It describes an inner healing
that took place on a retreat.
The person writes:

For the past eight months
I have been in psychotherapy,
a fact known to few people.
As a child I experienced overwhelming fear
because of hatred and abuse.

The details are unnecessary,
but much of the fear is centered on my mother.
I had become so turned off
to the concept of mothers
that I consciously rejected the love of Mary,
the mother of Jesus.

Yesterday,
after your talk on personal conversion,
I walked outside—feeling deeply alone.
I prayed for some kind of conversion
to help me break through the walls
that keep me from trusting.
I wanted to cry, but haven't in months.

You may have noticed
a small, round building near the cemetery.
Curiosity is one of my strongest traits—
I walked over to it and opened the door.
When I looked inside,
I was filled with fear.

There stood a large statue of Mary—
and my first impulse was to run away in anger.

───────────

But something drew me slowly to the kneeler
at her feet.

Then I fell on my knees,
weeping into the folds of her robes.

───────────

When it was over, I felt cleansed and new.
I felt willing to be a trusting child.

Even more important,
I felt that the love of a mother
had touched me—leaving in me a true desire
to forgive my natural mother.

───────────

Now, for the remaining ____ minutes,
just rest there,
realizing that God wants to heal you
of any inability you have
to forgive another person.

Devotional Paths

5 *You will show me
the path that leads to life.*
PSALM 16:11

Most of us
have a favorite prayer or poem.

It is one we enjoy reading over and over,
just as we enjoy listening to a favorite song
over and over.

This is what we mean
by a *devotional* prayer path.
It is a prayer or poem
that speaks to us in a special way.
It is one that we enjoy reading again and again.

A good way to use a devotional path
is the way backpackers use a path.
They stray from it occasionally
to look at a deer, a flower, or a view.

We should use devotional paths the same way.
We should feel free
to stray from them occasionally
to explore the feelings or thoughts
that they generate in our mind and in our heart.

Convict's Prayer

49

Imagine this scene.
A prisoner is on death row
at the Kentucky State Penitentiary in Eddyville.
His name is Jack Joe Holland, prisoner #30067.

As you watch,
Jack Joe kneels down, bows his head,
and prays aloud this prayer,
which he has just written:

Father,
I come to you a bent and broken man,
and humble myself before you
with no strength left to stand. . . .

———————

I come to you from prison,
from a place that's called death row,
and ask you to take pity, Lord,
on this convict's wretched soul. . . .

———————

Replace this hate with blessed love
and dry these tear-stained eyes;
have mercy on this awful man;
please hear his mournful cries.

———————

I'm sorry for all the grief
I've caused you and everyone;
forgive me, Lord,
for letting down your only Son. . . .

———————

So wash me, Lord, with your loving blood
that was spilled so long ago,
and welcome me unto thy bosom
and comfort this poor lost soul.

For the remaining _____ minutes,
just rest there in God's presence,
letting Jack Joe's prayer
sink into your heart
and become your prayer as well.

General's Prayer

50

One night,
while on combat duty in the Pacific Ocean,
General Douglas MacArthur wrote a prayer.

In it, he asked God to look after his son,
something he couldn't do
because he was so far from home.

(Though the prayer is for a son,
it is equally appropriate for a daughter.)

Now, listen to these excerpts from the prayer.
As you do,
imagine your own father or mother
praying them for you.

Build me a son, O Lord,
who will be strong enough to know
when he is weak,
[and] brave enough to face himself
when he is afraid. . . .

Build me a son whose wishes
will not take the place of deeds. . . .

Lead him, I pray,
not in the path of ease and comfort,
but under the stress and spur
of difficulties and challenges.

Let him stand in the storm;
let him learn compassion
for those who fall.

Build me a son whose heart is clear,
whose goals will be high;

a son who will master himself
before he seeks to master [others],
who will reach into the future,
yet never forget the past.

And after all of these things are his,
add, I pray, enough of a sense of humor
so that he may always be serious
yet never take himself too seriously. . . .

Then I, his father, will dare to whisper,
"I have not lived in vain."

Now, for the remaining _____ minutes,
just rest there, asking God to help you
become the kind of son or daughter
described in the general's prayer.

Jesus Dream 51

Imagine you have just awakened from a dream.
As you lie in bed fully awake,
the dream is still vivid in your memory.

In your dream it is Good Friday evening.
Jesus has just been buried.
You're standing in the shadow of an olive tree,
near the tomb,
which is a cave in a hillside.

Two torches are blazing brightly
on either side of the entrance to the tomb.
Two Roman soldiers with long spears
are marching back and forth
in front of the tomb.

Suddenly,
from the shadow of the olive tree,
you find yourself speaking to Jesus,
who lies lifeless inside the tomb:

*Lord, I hear Judas betrayed you with a kiss.
It hurts when friends turn against you.
Sorry I wasn't able to be there to support you.*

———————

*Lord, I hear your trial was a farce.
It hurts when witnesses lie about you.
Sorry I wasn't there to set the record straight.*

———————

*Lord, I hear you fell carrying the cross.
I can imagine how heavy it was.
Sorry I wasn't able to be there to help you.*

———————

Lord, I hear your friends left you on Calvary.
That's when you needed them most.
Sorry I wasn't able to be there to be with you.

Lord, I hear the crowd mocked you on the cross.
Death's hard enough as it is.
Sorry I wasn't able to comfort you.

Lord, if I just wasn't so busy,
I could show you that I really love you.
Sorry I have so much to do.   ANONYMOUS

Now, for the remaining ____ minutes,
just rest there, pondering the dream
and what God may be trying to say to you
through it.

Footprints

52

Imagine you are the person
who wrote the following words.
Try to experience in your imagination
everything the person did.

I dreamed
I was walking along the beach with the Lord,
and across the sky flashed scenes from my life.
For each scene
I noticed two sets of footprints in the sand;
one belonged to me, the other to the Lord.

When the last scene flashed before us,
I looked back at the footprints in the sand.
I saw that many times along the path of life,
there was only one set of footprints.
I also noticed that it happened
at the lowest and the saddest times in my life.

I questioned the Lord about it.

"Lord, you said that once I followed you,
you would walk with me all the way,
but I have noticed
that during the troublesome times in my life,
there is only one set of footprints.
I don't understand why,
in times when I needed you most,
you would leave."

The Lord replied,

*"My precious child, I would never leave you
during your times of trial and suffering.
When you see only one set of footprints,
it was then that I carried you."* ANONYMOUS

These words from Scripture come to mind:

*The Lord, your God, carried you,
as a man carries his child,
all along your journey.* DEUTERONOMY 1:31 (NAB)

Now, for the remaining _____ minutes,
continue to walk along the beach
with the Lord, enjoying his presence—
just as he enjoys your presence.

Dresser Card

53

Imagine you are the high school student
who wrote the following:

After my mother died,
I was bewildered and lost.
Everything in our house that she ever touched
became precious to me.

———————

One day I noticed a card
underneath the glass top of my dresser.
It had something written on it.

I recalled seeing the card for the first time
just after my mother went to the hospital.
But I didn't pay any attention to it then.
Now I pulled it out and read it.

———————

The writing said:

"For ev'ry pain we must bear,
For ev'ry burden, ev'ry care,
there's a reason.

"For ev'ry grief that bows the head,
For ev'ry teardrop that is shed,
there's a reason.

"For ev'ry hurt, for ev'ry plight,
For ev'ry lonely, pain-racked night,
there's a reason.

"But if we trust God, as we should,
It will work out for our good.
God knows the reason."

As I stood there, I could picture my mother
coming into my room
before she went to the hospital.
I could see her putting the card
underneath the glass top, as if to say,
"It's all right. God knows the reason."

I took the card and put it in my wallet.
Immediately a great peace came over me,
and I was able to accept my mother's death.

Now, for the remaining ____ minutes,
pick out something from your own life
that you don't understand.
Ask God to give you
the same understanding and peace
that he gave the student.

Sea Psalm

54

During World War II,
a military plane crashed in the Pacific Ocean.
Miraculously,
all eight members of the crew survived.
For twenty-one days
they floated in a rubber raft,
living on raw fish and rain water.

Each day
the crew members prayed together.
Their favorite prayer was Psalm 139.

Now imagine you're one of the survivors.
Picture yourself lying in the raft,
rocking back and forth in the water.
Everywhere you look, there's water.

Suddenly, everyone grows quiet,
and the captain of the crew
begins to pray Psalm 139
from his tiny pocket Bible.

As the captain prays, you fix your eyes
on a billowing white cloud in the sky
and listen to God's Word.
You listen to it
as you've never listened to it before:

Lord, you have examined me and you know me.
You know everything I do;
from far away you understand all my thoughts.

You see me, whether I am working or resting;
you know all my actions.

Even before I speak,
you already know what I will say.

The captain continues to pray from the Bible:

[Lord], you are all around me on every side;
you protect me with your power. . . .
Where could I go to escape from you?
Where could I get away from your presence?

Finally, the captain concludes, praying:

[Lord],
if I went up to heaven, you would be there. . . .
If I flew away beyond the east
or lived in the farthest place in the west,
you would be there to lead me,
you would be there to help me.   PSALM 139:1-5, 7-10

Now, for the remaining _____ minutes,
just lie there in the raft,
looking up at the vast blue sky,
realizing that God is also looking down on you.

Chris's Prayer

55

Imagine
you're the young person in this story.
The person's name is Chris.

Chris wants to fit in at school,
but she also wants to follow Jesus,
whom Chris believes to be the Son of God.

At times, Chris feels torn apart
between what's right and what's wrong.

One night Chris sits down,
picks up a pencil,
and composes this prayer to Jesus.
It comes from Chris's heart.

As you listen to the prayer,
let it sink into your own heart
and become your prayer as well.

Jesus, give me your light,
because sometimes I get confused
and it's hard for me
to know what's right.

Jesus, give me your courage,
because sometimes I feel pressured,
and it's hard for me
to do what's right.

Jesus, give me your love,
because sometimes I feel rejected,
and it's hard for me to keep loving.

Jesus, give me yourself,
because my heart was made for you
and it will not rest
until it rests in you.

Now, for the remaining ____ minutes,
just rest there,
listening with your heart
to what Jesus might want to say to you
in response to the prayer
that you've just made to him.

One Solitary Life

56

There's a poem called "One Solitary Life."
As you listen to it, try to picture
the remarkable person it describes. It reads:

Here was a young man
who was born in an obscure village,
the child of a peasant woman.

He worked in a carpenter shop
until he was thirty, and then for three years
he was an itinerant preacher.

He never wrote a book.
He never held an office.
He never owned a home.
He never had a family.
He never went to college.
He never set his foot inside a big city.
He never traveled two hundred miles
from the place where he was born.
He never did one of the things
that usually accompany greatness.
He had no credentials but himself.

While he was still a young man,
the tide of public opinion turned against him.
His friends ran away.
He was turned over to his enemies.
He went through the mockery of a trial.
He was nailed to a cross between two thieves.

While he was dying, his executioners gambled
for the only piece of property he had on earth,
and that was his coat.
When he was dead,
he was laid in a borrowed grave
through the pity of a friend.

Nineteen centuries have come and gone,
and he is still the central figure
of the human race
and the leader of the column of progress.

I am far within the mark when I say
that all the armies that ever marched,
and all the navies that ever sailed,
and all the parliaments that ever sat,
and all the kings that ever reigned,
put together, have not affected human life
upon this earth as has that One Solitary Life.

AUTHOR UNKNOWN

Now, for the remaining ____ minutes,
just rest there, realizing that this same Jesus
wants to enter your life and affect it,
just as he did the course of human history.

Faith Questions 57

Imagine that
you are beginning to question your faith.
Things you used to believe
have suddenly become hard to believe.
You don't know what's wrong.

You even wonder if God is abandoning you.

———————

One day, in desperation,
you visit the church that you grew up in.

You walk up the front steps,
open the big door, and enter.

Inside, everything is quiet and peaceful.

———————

After a minute or so,
you begin to walk around,
looking at all the familiar objects.

They bring back so many good memories.

———————

After looking around for a while,
you go up to the altar, kneel down,
and talk to Jesus about your faith.
You talk to him as you do to your best friend.

———————

You conclude your conversation with Jesus
by saying:

*Jesus, in spite of all my confusion,
I still believe four things with all of my heart.*

*I believe that you entered our world of sin
that we might change it into a world of love.*

*I believe that you embraced us
that we might embrace one another.*

*I believe that you understand us,
even though we don't understand ourselves.*

*I believe that you'll never turn away from us,
even though we may turn away from you.*

ANONYMOUS

―――――――――

Now, for the remaining ____ minutes,
just kneel there at the altar—
in the silence of the church—
listening with all your heart
for what Jesus might want to say to you
in response to your prayer to him.

Pilot's Card

58

Imagine you are the woman in this story.
Try to experience everything she did.

One day
an elderly woman was sitting in her room
in a nursing home.
She was staring out the window,
watching it rain.

———————

As she watched the tiny raindrops
trickle down the glass of her window,
she felt completely abandoned—even by God.

It was a terrible, lonely feeling.

———————

The elderly woman
rarely had a visitor anymore.
Both of her sisters were dead,
and her only son
was an Air Force pilot stationed in Europe.

———————

Just then, a nurse came into her room
with a letter from the woman's son.

As the elderly woman opened the letter,
a card fell from it into her lap.

She picked it up.
On it was written a prayer that said:

"Jesus, Lord of the elderly and the sick,
take my hand
when I am gray and feeble.

"Jesus, Lord of the aged and the depressed,
touch my hand
when I feel lonely and abandoned.

"Jesus, Lord of the flowers and the birds,
care for me
when I can no longer care for myself.

"Jesus, Lord of the lambs and flocks,
be with me
when I can no longer be with those I love."
                                          ANONYMOUS

When the elderly woman finished the prayer,
something entered her soul
and filled it with great peace.

Now, for the remaining _____ minutes,
just rest there,
sharing the peace that the woman felt
after reading the prayer on the card.

The Cross

59

There's a retreat house at Barrington, Illinois.
The retreat grounds are filled with trees.
Among the trees stands a stone cross
with a life-size body of Jesus hanging on it.

Now imagine you are the person
who wrote the following:

One night on my retreat at Barrington,
I was walking outside all by myself.
A light rain was falling.
I came upon the stone cross among the trees.
A spotlight was shining on it,
and water was trickling down the body of Jesus.
The sight of this moved me deeply.

I walked up to the cross
and rested my hand on it lovingly.
I felt unworthy to touch the body of Jesus.
As I stood there,
tears mixed with the rain in my eyes.

My thoughts turned to a card
in my wallet.
It was given to me years ago by my wife.
On the card are these words:

"I carry a cross in my pocket,
A simple reminder to me. . . .
This little cross is not magic,
Nor is it a good luck charm. . . .

"It's not for identification,
For all the world to see.
It's simply an understanding
Between my Savior and me. . . .

"It reminds me to be thankful
For my blessings day by day
And strive to serve him better
In all that I do and say. . . .
Reminding no one but me
That Jesus Christ is Lord of my life,
If only I let him be."

Now, for the remaining ＿＿ minutes,
just stand there in the rain,
with your hand resting on the cross,
asking Jesus to heal you
of whatever keeps you from letting him
be Lord of your life.

Tandem Bicycle

60

A young person was on retreat.
She told her small discussion group:

When I decided to follow Jesus more closely,
I thought my life would be smooth-sailing.
At first it was.
But then things got wild—really wild!

A good description of how my life changed
is the following poem.
It compares a life of following Jesus
to two people riding a tandem bicycle.

The poem begins:

"At first, I sat in the front; Jesus in the rear.
I couldn't see him, but I knew he was there.
I could feel his help when the road got steep."

The poem continues:

"Then, one day, Jesus changed seats with me.
Suddenly, everything went topsy-turvy.
When I was in control,
the ride was predictable, even boring.
But when Jesus took over, it got wild!
I could hardly hold on.
'This is madness!' I cried out.
But Jesus just smiled—and said, 'Pedal.' "

The poem concludes:

"And so I learned to shut up and pedal—
and trust my bike companion.

Oh, there are still times when I get scared
and I'm ready to give up.
But then Jesus turns around, touches my hand,
smiles, and says, 'Pedal.' "

The young person concluded
be telling her discussion group:

If you're somebody
who likes things quiet and predictable,
don't get mixed up with Jesus.
Above all,
don't switch seats with him on the bicycle.

Now, for the remaining _____ minutes,
just rest there, trying to imagine
how your life might change
if you suddenly got the faith and the courage
to switch seats with Jesus on the bicycle.